BUT GOD

He is the Author and Finisher of my Faith

Odessa Bradley

RELENTLESS
PUBLISHING

Published by :
Relentless Publishing House
www.relentlesspublsihing.com

RELENTLESS
PUBLISHING

ISBN: 978-1948829779

"This story is about a 6yr old girl who lost her mother and father to a life of poverty."

In Hickory, NC, three younger sisters and I were sent by our father to live with his grandmother who raised us. My mother walked out and left her seven children. My dad took care of us to the best of his ability. My father who didn't know the first thing about raising girls sent us down south to Hickory, North Carolina to live with his grandmother to show us the way of life. This way of life was not glamorous, but it was all my great-grandmother knew in the south to teach us. Our way of living changed dramatically. We went from being able to go to the bathroom inside our home, to having to use an outhouse. We went from running water to carrying water, heat at our fingertips to making heat to keep warm and cook with. I became accustomed to going to school with white and black children; to going to school with only black children. We had to share books because we could not afford our own books. The classes were so small. The second and third grade students were taught in the same room by the same teacher. When you passed one grade you just went to the other side of the room for the next grade. This new lifestyle didn't allow me to go into the stores; we weren't allowed to shop in the grocery or convenience store. We had to go around to the back of the store to the window and tell the attendant what my grandmother wanted. Back home with our dad, we were able to go where ever we wanted, but living in Hickory, we weren't privileged to do so. I was very unhappy living down south, and no matter how much I would beg my dad for us to go back up north with him, the answer was always no. I hated living in Hickory so bad. I remember running behind my dad's station wagon after every one of his summer visits. I truly believe had he known we had to carry water for over a mile back to the house, along with carrying coal and wood just to keep warm, he would have taken us back with him. My great-grandmother taught me everything. She taught me how to light a fire, how to cook and can fruits and vegetables. My auntie taught me how to plait my sister's hair. Being the oldest I had to take on the most responsibility. When someone was sick, my great-grandmother would go and pray healing over them. I would tag along with her reading the scriptures from the bible. My great-grandmother was a woman of God, this I know for sure. God kept us because of her. We stayed rooted and grounded in Him because she was a woman of God. She read the Bible twenty-four seven. She never formally learned to read or write, however she learned the word of God. As a child, I couldn't fathom how she knew the word and couldn't read a word. One day, as she and I were talking, I asked her, "How can you read the scripture if you don't know how to read?" She told me her husband was a minister and he could read. He would read the scriptures out loud daily and that is how she came to learn the scriptures. She learned where they were, the meaning and could quote them. Nobody but God could have brought us to her for safe keeping, to teach and instill the word of God in us. When I reflect on my life now, I ask myself if it had not been for her, where would I have been? If my father hadn't taken us down to her where would we have been? Only God knows what could have happened with seven kids. Social Services could have come in and split us up. My sister's and I could have ended up in a foster home that only God knows where. God gave my father a way out by telling him to take us south so that we could stay together. By him doing so, it prevented social services from coming and splitting us up. God kept me through it all. I kept a journal from age twelve about all the things that happened to me in Hickory, NC. Those journals were destroyed and lost, but I believe as long as you have breath in your body you still have time to share your story.

Great-grandmother believed in going to church. We walked every Sunday to church. She was the mother of the church and she loved it. I never realize how old she was at the time when it was announced she was the mother of the church. I asked her "Why, was she the oldest person in the church?" During that time my great-grandmother was in her 70's. I didn't think that was old, but I realize later that she was. That why when my aunt would do things she didn't like, my great-grandmother would just let it go. She always wanted to see all of her living kids before she died and she did. God granted her wish.

My sister and I was in the third and fourth grade, while my younger two sisters did not attend school. The youngest was only a year old. After school we would stop by the babysitters to pick them up before we walked the rest of the journey home.

I remember the day that changed our lives. One day

after school while at home, my youngest sister received third degree burns from hot cooking grease. After this happened my father thought it was best to take us to Hickory to live with our great-grandmother. Our older brothers, who were to walk us home and watch us, were not home. It felt like my brothers didn't seem to care much about us. Although they were young, they really wanted to do what they wanted without the responsibility of taking care of kids. As the oldest daughter I would make sure to get the others together after school, while we waited on our brothers to meet us and walk us home. When they didn't show up, I would just take my younger siblings and walk home. Stopping by the babysitters on the way to pick up the youngest children.

By the time we made it home, my brothers had already been there, and cooked dinner, but wasn't there to feed us. We saw that the food was already cooked, and we were hungry. We moved the frying pan to get to the food. I noticed the pan still had hot cooking grease in it. When we went to move the pan the handle turned and the hot grease poured out on to my sister who was crawling around on the floor. We didn't see her crawling around and she ended up getting burned. Being scared out of our minds all we could do is pray. I told my sister we needed to pray that someone will come. We wrapped her up in a blanket, because we didn't know what else to do. We watched my dad pray all the time for my mother to come home. As he prayed we prayed and prayed too. My dad came home early that day. It was God that brought him home because he would normally go to his second job everyday just to make ends meet. When he came home and saw what had happened he was so scared. He picked my little sister up looked her over. Then he noticed my other sister got burned too. He quickly took both of them to the hospital. My other sister and I stayed at home till my brothers came in from the day, we rushed to tell them what happened.

My brothers knew they were going to get a beating for not being at home. I knew I was going to get one too. When my father came home from the hospital with only one of my sisters, I knew my youngest sister had to stay in the hospital. My brothers got a beating for not being there with us. I believe if they were there we would still been in the north with our brothers, but because of that, we went south to my father's grandmother and my great-grandmother. He had no one to take care of us. My mother had two sister and they had children of their own. They had as many children as my mother did. One sister had seven and the other had six children. Every now and then my father would ask them to do our hair and watch us but I guess that got old. My aunts began to avoid my father's request for help with us. Helping us would stop them from going out to the bars and doing what they wanted to do even with their kids. When my dad picked my sister up from the hospital and she was healed, he took us to his grandmothers in Hickory, NC.

When we arrived in Hickory, NC I was in the third or fourth grade. I learned very quickly since multiple grades were in the same room, I would learn the next grade work while learning my own grade. I was naturally curious and eager to learn. By the time I was promoted to the next grade, I knew what to do. I remember we had to shop out of the goodwill from the backdoor of the shop. There was a little room we could go in to pick out some used shoes and clothes. We couldn't afford anything else. I was grateful for that.

When we went to the health clinic for glasses and our booster shots, I was the only one that had to get glasses. My eyes were so bad that I had to have drops put in my eyes daily. Every time my great-grandmother would tell me, "Pray over your eyes child. Pray that God would heal them." Being a child and having a childlike mind, I didn't know what she was talking about. I just said, "Yes mama," and I did what she told me every day. I still wear glasses but over the years my eyes did get better. I was wearing bifocal and now I wear single vision. My great-grandmother was right, God healed my eyes. For years I didn't have to have drops put in my eyes, and when I look back all I can say is nobody but God got us through.

My great-grandmother was my first impression of an entrepreneur. Like me, she would try to do a little bit of everything. She would heal people, pray for everyone, and take care of people. She would also sell or trade for wood and coal to heat and cook with. She would iron the white man shirts and sheets in trade for wood or coal. We had a washer on the back porch where we would wash our clothes and hang them on the clothesline outside. Then we had to iron them. When we ironed, we had to put the iron on the kitchen stove to get it hot. My great-grandmother would say, "Don't iron the tail of the shirt," and of course I wanted to know why. She said, "It would make the man mean." I would iron and fold them exactly how she taught me. When the customers would come to pick up their laundry, she would receive some coal or wood for her services. We would have to carry the wood to the back yard and put it under the porch. When I came home from school, I would hate to see the wood there because I knew we had to get it put under porch before dark.

In the summer time we would get peaches, bushels of peas, and tomatoes to can for the winter. My great-grandmother taught me how to can the vegetables. We also raised hogs. She would always call them hogs when it was time to kill them. We raised chickens and rose up early every morning to get the eggs. My great-grandmother would sell them to help bring money into the house. In the winter, she would kill a hog to make money. She would sell everything off that hog. She took the fat, cooked it and made lard to cook with. We had to make souse meat and liver mush. We also had to clean chittlins, which was not fun. She sold all three of these as well. One hog would make like four to five buckets of lard. The skins form the hog would be cooked in a black pot in the back yard. She would bag and sell the skins. My great-grandmother would sell everything off the hog. We would make all kinds of food from the hog; hams, pork lions, ribs, hamburger, fat back meat. My Uncle Hi would do all the meat for my great-grandmother and of course he would take whatever he wanted, and my great-grandmother wouldn't say anything to him.

My Uncle Hi is where we would get running water from. His house was in the city. We would carry the water from his home, anytime we needed water. We would get the water and bring it back to my great-grandmother's home before dark. We could not be out after dark. We used the water to cook, wash clothes, drink and everything else.

We also picked blackberries and crab-apples to can for the winter. My great-grandmother would cook a pot of soup that lasted all week. She would just open another jar of vegetable and put it into the pot. She taught me how to make yeast rolls and biscuits. I learned real quick how to cook for my sisters. This was just the start of my life in Hickory. I would have to bathe my sisters, comb their hair and press their clothes for school. When we went to school, I had to make sure we all went and came home together or I knew what would happen. We had a goat that would chase us if we wore red. That goat was crazy, but fun. We had a dog too, but our neighbor had bigger dogs. They were mean bulldogs. I think our neighbor used those dogs for fights. Whenever those dogs saw us coming home from school, they would try to attack us. We would run in the house just to get away from them. One day our neighbor's gate was opened and I said, "Oh, we better run and run fast before they gets us." I ran as fast as I could. I barely made it in the house but one of the dogs got my shoe. My great-grandmother knew it wasn't my fault. She went and bought me another pair of shoes. When you got a pair you better take care of them because with money being scarce, it was hard to know when we would get another pair. There were times I would put pieces of cardboard in my shoes so my feet would not be on the ground through the torn souls of my shoes or get wet from the rain.

My dad's sister was always mean to me. When we first came to stay there, my dad's sister would threaten to put a rat or a bug on me. My daddy's sister was mean and jealousy of us because we had hair and she didn't. We all stayed in the same room because we didn't have separate rooms of our own. We slept on a pull out sofa and there were times I was scared to go to sleep because she didn't wants us there. We would be sleeping in the bed and could look down and see outside through a crack in the floor. When we swept the floor we swept the dirt into the crack in the floor. I remember when my Aunt from New York would come down to visit us. She would also send us dolls for Christmas. My dad's sister would take the hair off the dolls head. There would be times we would come home from school and our dolls didn't have any hair. She would put the doll hair in her head. She could have become a millionaire if she would have patented it and start selling the hair, but instead she was only trying to be white, and have good hair like the dolls. I told my Aunt not to send us dolls anymore because my dad's sister was cutting the hair off their heads. Most years we didn't get anything for Christmas except a bag of oranges, apples nuts and candies, but we were happy to get that. When my Aunt would send us dolls or something from New York, we were so happy to receive it.

It was hard on us when my dad would come in the summer. He would bring us food for the house which would last for a long time. He would also bring us some shoes and we were so happy. We would always hope to go back north with him. As I reached my teenage years, I would go to work for my Aunt in the factory and go to clean house with my great-grandmother of this old white lady. She knew where everything in her home was. She would make me clean her toilet and tub, while taking a magnifying glass to see if I cleaned them. She would make me take all the can goods out of her cabinets, wipe them down and put all the can goods back. One day I took a can of pork and beans to add to the ones my aunt would buy on the weekend for me working with her at the factory. That old lady knew everything and told my great-grandmother I took a can of beans. I lied and said, "No, I didn't." because I did not to get a beating. To this day my great-grandmother never knew or she didn't let me know she knew. She just let me go to work with my Aunt to the factory. My dad's sister also worked at the factory too, and she would ask my great-grandmother if I could go with her too. She worked at night and on the weekends. We were both still in school. I think it was her last year. My other Aunt got her a job there. While working at the factory, they showed me how to put the sock on the machine and when it a came back around take them off. I got so good that I was making dozens of socks at a time. My Aunt Tie would tell me to slow down or we would be out of work. I did what she told me. I was not of age to work in there and I never got paid. My dad's sister and my Aunt did. She would bring us a can of pork and beans and hot dogs on Saturday for a real treat. We were so excited for the weekends because we got to eat hot dogs and pork and beans. Throughout the week it was soup, or beans and biscuits, or whatever my great-grandmother could make.

When I went to work with my dad's sister she started messing around with the boss's son. He was a white male. They would have me waiting in his car for hours while they were in a hotel room or in the office building upstairs. When I got home, my great-grandmother would say, "Work long today," and I would say, "Yes mama," that's because my dad's sister would threaten me not to say anything, so I didn't. She tried to be nice to me sometimes, but she had an evil spirit. My great-grandmother didn't see it. All my dad's sister had to do was give her a little money, a Pepsi and Goody Powder and she was satisfied. My dad and his sister lost their mother when she was around forty years old. My dad's sister would give me money sometimes. I thought she was being nice to me. She was married to a man from Louisiana. No one had ever seen him. She meet him and married him, but she was messing around with the boss's son. When she became pregnant and had the baby, the baby was born white. My great-grandmother was surprised, but told her that her husband was light skin. My great-grandmother said, "Okay." I am not sure if she believed her or not.

My dad's sister thought the baby would turn a little

dark, but he didn't. This went on for two years telling great-grandmother lies. She told her husband we had white people in our family. He finally came to visit and that's when everything hit the fan. She was done and he didn't want anything to do with her, because he knew the baby wasn't his. She was helping to pay for his college with the white man's money but he didn't know that. When the white man's father found out about the baby, he shipped his son so far away. She couldn't talk to him and couldn't find him anywhere. It wasn't until years later that she found out what the father did.

My dad's sister moved on with her life. She was jealous of us and didn't want us there. We were in her way with our great-grandmother. She couldn't get anything from our great-grandmother. She would tell her lies that we were here and there. One day she tried to run me down with her car because I told her I was going to tell great-grandmother on her. I started running, but I didn't make it in the house. She got out the car, and I knocked her down. We started fighting and my great-grandmother was yelling at me to stop, but I had enough! I wouldn't stop hitting her. I had her down and I was beating her, until my Uncle came outside with a gun and shot up in the air. At that moment, I stopped. I told my dad when he came to visit us. I told him how his sister was treating me and he got her good. He told her not to put her hands on me again. He said, "You working down here? Then I need to send for you in the summer and you can work up North." I was happy.

In 1965 the schools where integrated. We could go to the white school, but blacks still couldn't ride the bus. We had to walk to school. We could only walk on one side of the school, and sit on one side of the building at lunch. While in the classroom my teacher would ask me how I had so many credits. It was because I was a quick learner and I wanted to get out of school so I could go back home up North with my dad. My great-grandmother was good and she protected us from things, but I just wanted to go home.

When I turned sixteen, my dad sent for me. I rode the Greyhound bus to get a job up North at a nursing home. I made $96 dollars every two weeks and that was great. I thought I was rich. My dad instructed me not to cash my check, but to wait on him to help me open a savings account for me. This was so I would have the money when I go back South, but I didn't want to go back South. He told me someone had to see about my sisters. When it was time to go back South, my dad would let me go to the store to get some clothes, coats and shoes for my sisters and myself. I was glad I could spend money on my sisters, because I didn't want us to look so poor even if we were poor. When I got home, I was determine that we would have our own books for school. We would have to pay for our books and this time I had the money pay for our books. My great-grandmother would try to preach the little money I had out of my hands. I would still go buy what we needed at the back door of the store.

This particular day I told the man I wanted a six pack of Pepsi, Goody powder and two boxes of snuff for my great-grandmother. He would say, "Do you have the money for this," and I responded, "Yes sir, I do." He said, "Okay girl." When I got back to Hickory with my Dad, I was glad to see my sisters and I know they were glad to see me.

My Uncle would volunteer to go to the store for my great-grandmother and I would give him some money, and he would ask if I could go with him. I did not think anything would go wrong being he was my uncle and a Christian man who sings in the all male choirs in the church. As we were going to the store, he tried to kiss me and put his hands under my dress. I jumped out of his truck and he begged me to get back in the truck or he would be in trouble. I did and when I returned back home my great-grandmother knew something happened. My Uncle gave his own self away by saying nothing happened. He was scared my great-grandmother would tell my auntie, and she would put him out of her house. He was suppose to be a Christian, but he was the devil. All I saw of that man was him running the women in the church. I would always hear other women trying to meet up with him. I would tell my auntie, but she didn't believe it, so I left that alone. I never told my children what happen to me in Hickory because I try to bock that out of my life.

One day my auntie beat my sister because she didn't come home with us after school. I told my sister to come, but she wouldn't. When they found her she got a beating and it was bad. My aunt would have to stop, sit down, rest, and then get up to finish beating her. She wouldn't cry at all. I cried for her and told her to cry, but she was not going to do it. Shortly afterwards my auntie stopped beating her. When my dad visited that summer, I told him what happen and my Aunt had been treating me. He told her if she ever put a hand on any of us again, she would be sorry. My dad was a big man and he meant every word he said. My auntie never put her hands on us again.

My cousin came down from New York with his mother and father. They wanted him to be raised in Hickory too. He was my great-grandmother son's child. They sent her money for him every two weeks so he received better treatment than us. We only had two bedrooms, a kitchen and living room. We were already sleeping on a pull out sofa and live in the same room with my dad's sister. Where was he going to stay? My aunt took him in and he stayed down stairs with her son and husband. My aunt built rooms in the basement for her, her son, and husband to live. She tried to control us, but that didn't happen after we told our dad what she was doing. She would make me go to work and never paid me. At the time I didn't know anything about getting paid. She would give my great-grandmother money to keep her from saying anything about me going to work with her on the weekends. I thought I was helping my great-grandmother out so I just did as I was told. When it was time to go to people's houses with my great-grandmother for her to pray and heal their bodies, I would quietly go. I did what she always told me to do, rub the oil down their bodies as she prayed. She made the oils and sometimes they would not smell good. I still had to rub it on them.

Sometimes they would have sores and burns. My great-grandmother would wrap their bodies and she would pray. She would pray for hours, and days until they were healed. I would say, "They're healed grandmamma," and she said, "Nothing but the grace of God." It wasn't her. It was always God. She would say, "Only God can do it. Just remember, He is the way, the truth and the light and no one can do what God can do. Remember, trust in Him and He will see you though." As a kid I did take it for granted and said, "Yes ma. Yes ma," but now I look back and she was right. Nobody but God will see you though.

There was a time I had sores on my body, and the health department doctors would say they didn't know how to treat me. My great-grandmother would say, "Okay, God can." She would pray for my healing. I would only breakout in the summer. I think it was because of the picking black berries in the woods, crab-apples, and tomatoes for canning. I never knew why I would breakout only on my legs, but she would make a cream and put it on my legs. It would heal them. I was exposed to everything including people being sick that my great-grandmother took me around.

Everyone in the neighborhood would call for Mama Addie. My great-grandmother's name was Mama Addie.

Everyone including the white men, who she would clean and iron their laundry. She had one son in prison. We would go visit him twice or maybe three times a year. It was in the mountains of North Carolina. We couldn't go in, but we would sit outside for hours waiting for her to come out the gate. He would send things home like a purse or handbag that they made in prison. My great-grandmother would sell them and send him money. Sometimes she would send money that my dad would send for us. She would also use the money my dad sent to get her other son, that's always getting drunk, out of jail too. She prayed that she would live to see all of her living children before for she died, and God granted her wish. She was a least 90 years old but they had to roll it back to 89 on the death certificate for the insurance company to pay the policy and it still wasn't enough. Her children along with my father still had to pay some money for her funeral expenses.

I left Hickory, NC, and my sisters before my great-grandmother passed away. We were her only great grandchildren. My father did the best he could for all seven of us. I was angry for years, until I realized that my dad sent us to Hickory for our good. When my mother walked out and left all seven of us with our father, he tried everything he could to take care of us by himself. He worked two jobs in order to send money to take care of us. He would come visit us every summer and He made sure we hand plenty of clothes and food. Even with all he done for us, while we lived in Hickory, there would be times it wasn't enough. Sometimes I would not eat just to make sure my sisters had something eat.

It was time for me to graduate from Hickory High School. I was glad I was leaving Hickory and going back home with my dad. I was the only child that graduated from that school. My sisters didn't stay long after I left Hickory. My dad sent for my sisters one by one until they all were back home up North. When I was close to graduation, my teacher asked me how did I earn so many credits. I told her I took everything I could because I didn't want to go home to work hard every day. I would tell my great-grandmother I had homework to do. Sometimes it worked and other times it didn't. I was offered a scholarship to a college in Charlotte, North Carolina, but I didn't accept the scholarship. I wanted nothing else to do with the south, I just wanted to go home. I got a job at the hospital where my dad worked. I was so happy to be back home with my dad.

I finally saw my mother for the first time since I was

a little girl. I didn't know who she was. I only remembered she was a light skin woman. When I met her, she never told me she was sorry nor if she missed us. Of course this made me angry. One day I asked her why she left us. She told me she wanted to live her life like her sisters. She also said my dad was mean and only wanted her to work. I didn't believe what she was saying about my dad. The man she was with at the time was a drunk, demanding, and mean. She invited me to come stay with her some time. I agreed to finally go live with her so I could get to know my mama but that didn't last for long. Her boyfriend was a drunk and a pervert. I was sleeping on her couch and he was trying to see if I was sleep. I moved and he went upstairs. He was angry with my mama. I heard him and I went up to their room with a gun and told him if he puts his hands on my mother I would kill him. The next day my mother told me I had to leave. I did and went back home with my dad. I saw she didn't care about me. One day I when I was living with her and she wasn't home at the time, the neighbors told me she was in the bar across the street. I went to the bar and she was there drinking a beer. She told me to leave and she would come on later. She said, "Just go to the house!" I saw how she drank just like her sisters did. I could remember when my dad would take us over to their house and they would be drunk. You could see the beer cans all over the house. My dad didn't tell me anything about my mother. I guess he wanted me to see for myself what kind of woman my mother was. She didn't care about us, only herself. I knew that I had to move on with my life.

I continued living with my dad and working. One day my sister came and told me she ran away from home. She called my dad and told him she was not going back to Hickory and I was so happy to see her. My other sisters was not as old as we were, but when they got tired of living that life in Hickory, they came home too. By that time, I was on my own and had moved out of my dad's home. I met my husband and moved in with him. I was eighteen and he was twenty at the time. We had to go to Maryland to get married because he had to be twenty-one in Pennsylvania to get married. This was the start of a new life for me. It wasn't always the best, but better than where I came from, But God.

Acknowledgments

This book is written for my grandchildren and great-grandchildren. I want them to see how being grateful that they have a grandmother that was so determined to make it and not to give up in the spirit of life. I lived in Hickory, North Carolina, with the only grandmother I knew. She was my great-grandmother and my mother. I want my grandchildren to know who I am and how much I love each one of them. Be blessed and live the right way. Try not to be resentful, be a good person, do not be envious of others, and love one another as a family. Continue to keep God in your life and He will get you through anything. I pray God grants me to live to see all of my grandchildren, great-grands, and great great-grandchildren as my great-grandmother did. Thank you great-grandmother, Mama Addie.

About the Author

I always was a writer and I loved to write.

I would think of things to do. I love to sew and helping people.

My goal in life is to please other before self.

www.ingramcontent.com/pod-product-compliance
Lightning Source LLC
Chambersburg PA
CBHW070050070426
42449CB00012BA/3223